Finding Your Way Through Work

Kathleen Marvin

CONTENTS

INTRO

Whether you hate your job or love your job, things could always be better. You wish you could change the people around you, or change the culture you're in – sometimes you think maybe you should change your whole life. Pretty much the only thing you have any chance of actually changing is yourself, which in fact would affect your whole world. It can be valuable to have a coach to support and facilitate your efforts to make changes, but that's not always possible.

The purpose of this guide is to assist you in making some changes to improve your experience at work, which incidentally, almost always improves the rest of your life as well. In my eight years of coaching people in the workplace, I've identified a few classic fundamental problems that most people encounter. I've addressed them here in an attempt at clarity and brevity because I know you're busy, with some suggestions about what you can do in these situations. I suggest keeping a journal, or at least taking a few notes about what's going on with you at work while you're reading this.

There's a certain amount of unnecessary suffering at work that can be alleviated by gaining more insight into the problems you confront and developing more sophisticated skills to deal with them. But first you have to be willing to take a good long look at yourself, which is always uncomfortable, and then you have to be sincerely willing to make some changes. This may seem daunting at first, but it can be quite interesting to experiment with different ways of doing things and exhilarating to see positive results from your efforts.

The question is, can people change? Or maybe the real question is, do you *believe* people can change? Most of us agree that we can evolve to a point, but after a certain age it becomes more difficult to imagine important change in ourselves and in our lives. The very act of coaching presumes that change is possible in the way you see things and the way you do things. And maybe that's where real change starts.

Neuroscientists have in recent years established that the brain has more plasticity and therefore ability to adapt than previously thought. Contrary to previous beliefs, adult brains can develop new neurons, and even damaged brains can regenerate. Although neuroscience is in early stages, it's becoming clear that there's evidence to support the idea that what an individual focuses on over time can literally change his physical brain. In short, yes, we can change, but we usually don't much want to. The familiar generally feels safer; the unknown a little frightening. Often we have to be in pain to be motivated to change the way we do things, or simply want something so badly we're willing to take the chance. My hope is that this guide can at least point you in the right direction so you can make your own way through to more comfort and satisfaction in your work.

At work we all have tasks, projects, and deadlines, and there is a strong tendency to believe that work is all about achieving these goals successfully – or at least appearing to. The question is how do these things actually get done? Certainly very little that you achieve is done all by yourself. It seems that almost nothing can be accomplished without the support or at least cooperation of other human beings. This reality implies that learning how to work with others to maximum mutual benefit probably has more value than anything else you do at work.

How can you learn to work smoothly and effectively with so many different people, especially when there's always at least one who drives you crazy? You start by paying at least as much attention to the people as you do to the task at hand. And that includes yourself. In fact, start with yourself. I was trained in integral coaching, in which the coach works with the whole person and not just a set of goals. The entire first six months of the program were dedicated to getting a deeper understanding of ourselves – our perspectives, proclivities, attitudes, and beliefs to prepare us to begin to coach others. It's important to take a good look at yourself and what it takes for you to change so you can better understand what's going on with those around you.

When you begin to observe yourself at work – the actions you take, the ways you communicate, and the interactions you have with colleagues, you start to get some ideas about how you might do things differently and get better results. At the same time, looking at yourself this way causes you to also take a deeper look at the people you work with and can lead to a better understanding of how to work with them more effectively.

While integral coaching is holistic in nature, addressing a client's intellectual, psychological, emotional, and physical well-being, as a coach I've chosen to focus on the work arena because work is a microcosm that provides all the challenging situations you encounter in your larger world. It's a great laboratory for experimenting to find better ways to achieve your goals and increase your happiness, and the stakes are high, which can stimulate rapid learning. I also like coaching people about work because it has clear context and constraints, and feels safe to clients once trust has been established. Good coaching helps the client find his or her own solution, which in my experience usually involves learning and personal growth

However, I believe you can make a lot of progress on your own if you're highly motivated. This guide presents ideas for you to consider, and recommends actions you can take to enhance your interpersonal skills so you can succeed with more ease and have more fun doing it. You probably spend most of your waking hours working. Why not find a way to do it better and enjoy it more?

ALL ABOUT ME

The gems of wisdom I offer you in this little guide may still be tinged with traces of blood, sweat, and tears, because I'm one of those people who have to learn things the hard way. I like learning how to do things by doing them, which means I learn from my mistakes, and have made plenty of them. And I've observed others making their own mistakes and paid attention to the results. I'm still always learning, because it gives my life meaning, and hope I never need to stop. I want to share some of my hard-won treasure with you.

I didn't have a career in my twenties, unless wandering the world seeking the answer to the mystery of life can be considered a career. I taught English as a Second Language, although I had no qualifications other than speaking the language. It gave me an opportunity to meet different kinds of people in different cultures, to learn a few languages, and to become highly skilled in getting by on almost nothing. At the end of that decade I returned to the U.S. with a little daughter thinking maybe I did need some kind of a career.

I started out doing grant writing for nonprofits, believing that was morally superior to becoming a cog in a corporate machine. However it soon became clear that I needed a little more profit and a little less "non", so I decided to see what I could do about it, even if it meant risking my soul. Almost by accident, I stumbled into a little software startup in the early eighties and was pleasantly astonished to see people sitting around in jeans and sneakers eating pizza and drinking Coke, all together in a large open space. It wasn't long before I figured out that nearly anything I could figure out how to do there, I could do there, and for the first time I felt my ambition ignited in relationship to work. As a single parent it was pretty much all about getting more money.

I became a technical project manager and when that place went belly up, moved on in that same role to another local startup that some of us referred to fondly as "the evil robotics company", which also eventually died, but was not mourned. A friend of mine got me a job interview at Autodesk, which at the time was still fairly small, but was a real company and was doing well. Somehow I convinced the hiring manager that I was a technical writer and got the job, which was pretty scary at first since I had no idea what technical writers did. Long story short, I decided I would be a lot better at managing than at being a technical writer and as there was no real technical publications Department at Autodesk at the time, volunteered to build one and to manage it.

I hired some smart and talented people (I was the hiring queen – when you don't know how to do much yourself, you need to be very good at finding the right people to work with you.) Together we created a world-class technical publications function and made ourselves proud. However we made so many changes to the way things had previously been done that I came to be viewed as a menace by a few people in high positions. I decided it would be prudent to seek new pastures, and probably more interesting, since techpubs was up and running. I wanted to find out what could be done about the fact that it was taking six months to get the products translated into other languages and created a job to do just that, taking with me a trusted colleague and friend who could actually implement good ideas, as opposed to just having them which I saw as my job.

We also thought it might be fun to be able to get out of the country once in a while. We connected with the bright and gracious translation manager in the Swiss office and with her developed new ways of working that allowed European products to ship very shortly after the American ones did. We spent a lot of time in Neuchâtel, Switzerland and went to Amsterdam, Barcelona, Paris, Munich, and Milan. We worked long hard hours, but we were highly engaged in figuring out how to make things work better.

Although technology doesn't particularly interest me, the technology business has been a great gift for me that allowed me to eventually function at the director level and to learn how people interact and organizations operate while working at Autodesk,

Apple (Claris), Adobe systems, and Sun Microsystems. Yes, it involved a lot of work and could be pretty frustrating at times, but learning to work under pressure in a rapidly changing environment with many different kinds of people all over the world ultimately forged me into an effective, mature professional (most of the time.)

Sun was big enough and loose enough to allow me to try something new again, so I moved from localization into sales operations, about which I knew nothing and which I pray I may never again have to do in this or subsequent lifetimes. But it was good to learn new things, and once again I got to put together a great little group of highly competent people who actually knew what to do from Korea, Japan, China, and the U.S. and traveled to Beijing, Bangkok, Tokyo, and Seoul.

About ten years ago, with my daughter very successfully matriculated from graduate school with a profession and a job, I asked myself this question – what do you *really* want to do? I thought about my kind of accidental career and asked myself which parts of it I had loved. While I like establishing new ways of doing things and solving problems, much more fascinating to me was trying to understand what was going on between people. I also came to enjoy developing and mentoring others, and got great pleasure watching so many of the intelligent and skilled people I had hired evolve and become more successful. So I thought, if that's your favorite thing, why not just do that, and only that.

In 2003 I completed a year-long intensive training to

become a coach at New Ventures West, a coaching school with an excellent program in integral coaching – meaning that you are always aware as a coach that you are coaching the whole person, trying to help them evolve in their work and in their lives. I did this to prepare myself for my next career while simultaneously working at Sun.

Then I left corporate life to focus exclusively on career coaching and in the eight years that I've been coaching have found this work to be by far the most satisfying and interesting of any professional endeavor I have ever undertaken. I find it completely absorbing and love the fact that it demands both intuition and analysis and requires an honest, sincere and deep interaction between the client and the coach to effect change. This constant exploration into what makes each person tick and what will allow them to grow and develop and become more successful, but above all happier, is an endless mystery and my great pleasure. Working closely this way with people on some of the things that are most important to them lets me feel like I can help make a difference, help make things better. Most of all I love the moments of revelation, which do come, when the right questions are asked.

I decided to go to graduate school to take a deeper look at what's really going on inside organizations and thus got my Masters in Organizational Psychology in 2008. I think it was the first time I truly enjoyed school – maybe I was finally old enough. After all those years of observing cultures and behaviors in different companies, it felt good to delve into theory; not to mention to validate many of my reflections on what I had experienced. I also thought it would be useful to my coaching clients to be able to see their own situations from an organizational perspective as well as a personal one.

In search of the true, essential value of coaching, I have actively sought as much diversity in my clients as possible, to better understand what they have in common and what they need. I've coached both corporate and nonprofit clients, executive directors, vice presidents, directors, managers, individual contributors, hospital janitors, and cooks at Google. I've coached people from Russia, Italy, France, Mexico, Korea, Thailand, Vietnam, India, the Philippines, and of course the U.S. While each client is unique and each coaching program must be developed with that in mind, there are certain issues that arise again and again, seemingly in almost any environment, and I've chosen the primary ones for this guide.

I believe that coaching can be an inspiring and even healing process and can help people improve their lives. For that reason I feel strongly that coaching should be available to anyone who wants it, and not remain an expensive luxury dedicated to executives. I wrote this guide to assist those who can't afford a coach right now, and to give a better idea of what coaching is for those who can.

This guide is short because I made every effort to communicate as clearly as I could with as few words as possible. I did this because I'm personally tired of skimming through books looking for the parts that are valuable to me, and wanted to create something that gets straight to the point and just gives you the good stuff. I hope you'll see it that way too and can get something for yourself out of it.

DO YOU FEEL LIKE ALL YOU DO IS WORK?

When we take full advantage of all the possibilities life has to offer, our minds, our hearts, and our energy work together harmoniously, opening us to the full richness of life, the deep enjoyment of experience.

Tarthank Tulku "Skillfull Means"

Do you ever find yourself sitting down to get some work done on a Sunday and realize that you have no specific project or task in mind? It's just that you always work on Sunday afternoons, oh and Saturday mornings, Tuesday evenings, and well pretty much every weekday evening after working all day. It's what you do; what you've done for years. Do you ever ask yourself why? The real answer might surprise you.

Yes, maybe you always have way too much to do, and it can't be accomplished in a normal work week. But why is that? Is your company in trouble and you have been led to believe that you have to do the work of three people? Is it because you don't know for sure what's expected of you, and are trying to cover all the bases? Is it because you're disorganized, and it takes a long time to put all the pieces together? Or do you need to be working all the time to feel productive, to feel safe, to justify your existence?

When you fear for your livelihood, it makes you feel safer to do nothing but work, because surely if you do nothing but work, no one will let you go. However, I think we've seen with great clarity in the past few years that this theory doesn't hold up. In fact what usually happens if you over-work out of fear (rather than desire), is that you burn out and become less effective, in spite of long hours and weekends with your nose to the grindstone.

Making work the top priority in your life and doing mostly only that is a beautiful escape. You can avoid a myriad of other responsibilities with the "I have to work" sledgehammer. After all, who in our society can argue with that? You don't have to make dinner, take the kids to the park, or even exercise. As an added benefit, you also don't have the time for all the creative endeavors you tell yourself you would undertake if only you didn't have to work all the time - taking a class in Indian cuisine, writing a poem, getting a ship into a bottle. You don't need to try new things at which you might fail.

Be honest with yourself. Do you really have to work this much or is it a habit? Are you being strategic with the time you spend working, identifying what's really important as well as knowing when you are most productive? You're a multi-faceted human being, with multiple needs and obligations, and when you allow yourself to become one-dimensional, some parts of you wither and die. Our culture makes it too easy to do nothing but work and consider it virtuous, so you have to look deeper to understand your own motives and figure out what's best for you and yours. The easy way out is to just keep working.

The trouble with losing yourself in your work is that you can lose your real self. In those rare moments when you find yourself alone and thinking about who you used to be, or who you thought you were anyway, it's easy to wax nostalgic for that potential pro baseball player, novelist, competitive swimmer. Everything seemed possible then, and thoughts of the future filled you with impatience to discover who you were meant to be. Now it feels like that was a different person.

Some of the things you loved to do are still part of the person you are now, even if you haven't done them for a long time; even if you might not set the world aflame when you do get back to them. And you may have new interests too, but no time to indulge. One way or the other, you need to be more than the sum of your obligations. This becomes crystal clear when events catapult your life into a whole new dimension – for example losing your job. Possibly just as frightening as losing your financial stability is the loss of identity you can experience when this happens. Without this job, who am I?

Build a more expansive framework for yourself so that regardless of what life throws at you, you will know who you are. Develop interests and activities for your personal pleasure and growth and insist on including them in your life, even though it's hard to squeeze them in. That way when you find yourself without a job, moving to another place, working through family difficulties, or just looking for meaning, you have something of value that's part of you that you can hold onto, and take with you if necessary. When the stiff breeze of the unexpected blows your way you can write something, or sit down at the piano, or go outside and play and know you'll get through it all. Find a way to always be able to remember who you really are.

Remember the fundamental and therapeutic experiences that can grace your life. Nature is still all around you, although you may have to make an effort to get into it, slow down, and feel it. Living in your body and not just your head is also quite helpful. Your body wants to move around and experience sunshine and fresh air, – to be part of the real world.

Positive psychology has developed only in the last ten years or so with the idea of identifying strengths and building on them to increase happiness. Positive psychology has reinvigorated a powerful tool that has been around since the beginning of time in most religions - the value of practicing gratitude. Identifying that for which you are grateful improves your state of mind, your degree of satisfaction with your life, and even your health. To be effective, a gratitude practice needs to be specific and consistent. Once begun, experiencing gratitude becomes easier and easier, until it becomes part of your everyday awareness.

Food tastes better when you realize how lucky you are to have something good to eat; the flowers in your garden are more fragrant when you are thankful for their beauty. Your home means more when you appreciate the shelter and environment it provides. Your body is a miracle because it tries so hard to continue to function well for you in spite of all you put it through. Most importantly, expressing gratitude to others can greatly improve relationships and spread the happiness. Expressing gratitude for the precious small gifts in your life can lift you up, and others with you.

Work can be a very good thing, especially if you're lucky enough to have work you like and care about. But it can't be the only thing if you want to really live your life. It takes determination and courage to hold on to this so you can hold on to yourself.

Things You Can Do

- You are most creative and efficient when you have your best energy, so design your work plan around those times and set a limit on your total hours.

- Prioritize so you can accomplish the most important tasks.

- Take short breaks – if possible go outside.

- Find something to do outside of work that's engaging, challenging, interesting, and fun. Take piano lessons again, start swimming a couple times a week, join a writers group, volunteer at your favorite non-profit, play on an ultimate Frisbee team.

- Do something that feeds you spiritually, like reading that elevates your perspective, meditating, or going to your place of worship.

- Keep a gratitude journal - jot down a few things you are grateful for just as you get up in the morning, or just before you go to bed. Write an email or simply tell someone you're grateful for certain things they do, or ways they are.

- Test your happiness quotient at Authentic Happiness.

- Begin thinking about what kind of work you want next so you can get ready. Mysteriously, preparing for a better future always makes the present more tolerable.

FINDING FOCUS

Far more than you may realize, your experience, your world, and even your self are the creations of what you focus on.

Winifred Gallagher, "Rapt"

There are millions of things you could be doing, seeing, reading; you have to make choices constantly. What you're letting in is becoming part of who you are, altering the way you see things and even the structure of your brain. Neuroscience has established the concept of neuroplasticity, the ability of adult brains to change, and studies have proven that experience literally alters brain structure.

There's a lot going on these days. In 1960 phones were connected to walls, movies were in theaters, music played on records, and nobody had a personal computer. Imagine life without the internet. Then there were three billion people in the world; now there are nearly 7 billion. Needless to say there is a lot more noise now.

The technology that was meant to free us for more leisure has trapped many of us in a world where we can work all the time. We are always connected, there are no excuses to be inaccessible, and people, problems and information are incoming day and night. With so much happening all the time, it's easy to over-caffeinate, stress out, and lose track of what's important.

This is true in every aspect of your life, including work. If you stop and listen to your mind as if you were merely an observer, rather than believing that it *is* you, it's kind of frightening. Buddhists call it "monkey mind" - leaping from branch to branch and chattering away, jumping from your to-do list to your bank account to something a colleague said to you yesterday to wondering if your next vacation should be in Hawaii or Italy. While you can't control many of the events and most of the people, you can do something about your response to all this stimuli.

It can be a relief to rein in that babble and focus on work, concentrating on the task at hand. Even then it takes deliberate intention to stay put until you accomplish one thing before you move on to the next, and it's easy to kid yourself into believing you can juggle four or five things at once. There are lots of forces pulling on you for your attention, and sometimes it's hard to know what has the most value.

A Stanford study shows that multitasking reduces your effectiveness dramatically, contrary to your impression that you can handle it all. When you're talking to someone on the phone, just do that - don't do email at the same time. Picture the person you're talking to, and listen to what they're saying. The conversation will be shorter, the person will feel heard, and you can move on. If you need to do something that requires thought, block out some time for it and get it done. It will be higher quality and take less time.

Try to live in the present moment, which can keep you calm and grounded. Most of the time we're not really here, but are instead reliving a past event or anticipating a future experience. Do whatever you're doing, and nothing else. Right now, what do you hear? What do you smell? What do you see? This focus isn't easy, and you'll constantly lose your concentration, but keep pulling yourself back to the attempt. In time your skill will increase, along with your mental power. You'll actually get more done, and do it better. You'll also create stronger connections with your colleagues, partners, and clients, and a source of renewable energy for yourself.

Make a few conscious decisions about where you want to focus in your life too while you're at it. Only you know what would be good for you, make you feel stronger, more flexible, more alive. Find a way to meet some new people who do different things than you do. Take a class to learn about something you have always wondered about. Get yourself into nature, spend more time with your dog. Carve out a space to be alone once in a while somewhere quiet. Paint a painting, cook a meal, sing a song. Read a few pages of something inspirational every day that uplifts you. Think about what you want to be more of, put yourself in its path, and pay attention. And every once in a while, whatever you are doing, stop. Breathe, look, smell, feel. The present moment is all we really have.

Things You Can Do

- Ask yourself what really needs to happen next. Shift your priorities as needed when conditions shift.

- Manage the interrupt mode by turning off audio alerts on email and texts and filtering instant messages. How often do you REALLY need to check – is it every hour, every 30 minutes? Do you seriously have to respond every couple of minutes to a new request or problem? (Unless, of course, you work in an intensive care unit.)

- Focus on the person who's actually in front of you over those who are trying to reach you via technology.

- Carve out some quiet time to be alone – take a daily walk or try a little meditation. Even 15 minutes can get you back to yourself and the present moment.

Simple Sitting Meditation

Find a comfortable, quiet place where you can either sit on a cushion on the floor or in a chair. It's good if your spine is straight.

Start by taking 3 slow, deep breaths.

Then breathe normally, focusing on your breath. You can think "breathe in" when you breathe in, and "breathe out" when you breathe out if you like.

No need to try to stop your thoughts. Just let them pass through and don't follow them.

When you find yourself getting lost in thought, bring yourself back to the present by returning to focusing on your breath. Even five minutes is good, and when you want to, you can begin to go longer. It can take a while to settle down and get calm and focused so there is benefit to going longer when you feel ready to do that.

It's very powerful to do this every day if possible. Good times are either early mornings or before going to bed. But just doing it is the important thing, when you can.

THE VOICES IN YOUR HEAD

What would it be like if I could accept this moment –
exactly as it is?

Tara Brach, "Radical Acceptance"

We all hear voices in our heads. The crazy part is how wildly different the messages are depending on the situation, the day, the moment. There is the voice of total futility – "why are you even bothering; there's no point; no one appreciates it anyway." There's the maniacally inflated voice – "you're awesome; you rock, you are better than absolutely everyone else." And perhaps worst of all that astonishingly angry and abusive voice who talks to you as you would never speak to anyone else – "what is the matter with you? You're an idiot, a fraud."

Some days you feel smart, strong, capable of whatever may come your way, and happily launch yourself into your work. Then there are those times when you feel totally inadequate, unqualified – an imposter. You're just not good enough. It's kind of frightening how suddenly this switch can go on or off. And yet in both modes you are exactly the same person.

The question is, what's good enough? And how can you find the equilibrium to feel like you're good enough most of the time, maybe even all the time? It helps to remember that this condition is true for almost everyone, with the exception of those who are so egocentric that they can avoid self-doubt altogether (and make the rest of us crazy.)

Some successes can be measured, but others are harder to identify. If you can't do it with numbers, you rely on those around you to acknowledge your achievements and treat you like a winner. However, there are circumstances where you just don't have the luxury of an adoring crowd applauding you – maybe you work alone as a consultant or contractor, or work someplace where recognition and respect are hard to come by. It's important to learn to support and congratulate yourself when there's no one else to do it for you.

First look at the standards you've set for yourself. Are they reasonable, achievable? Or are they almost impossible to meet? It's fine to have stretch goals, to take some calculated risks, but most of what you want to achieve should actually be possible within your environment. It's good to have ambitious aspirations, but important to break them down into incremental, achievable goals. You will make mistakes, that is if you're learning anything, so it's important to learn to acknowledge the mistake, figure out what it taught you, and quickly forgive yourself. Recognize your small successes as they move you toward the higher-level ones. Of course you have certain obligations that come with your job, but you can also define success on your own terms, based on what matters to you and measures up to your values.

Hopefully you will always have at least one goal that allows you to learn. It's critical to recognize when you are on a learning curve, and where you are on that curve. Many people confuse learning with incompetence, and panic just at the time when they most need to stay focused and absorb new information. When you feel like you don't know what you're doing, ask yourself if you're on a learning curve toward some new expertise. If the answer is yes, think about where you are on that curve. The beginning is probably the most difficult, since you are not yet certain exactly what you will need to learn or how long it will take, and usually you have to function and produce while still learning.

Knowing what circumstances are ideal for you to learn can help you find work that leverages your strengths. It can also explain why some situations make you feel like you're banging your head against a brick wall. Instead of beating yourself up when you're feeling like there's something wrong with you because you just don't get it, remember it's quite possible that the way you are expected to learn under the circumstances is just not the way you learn things. The Kolb Learning Style Inventory identifies four phases in the learning cycle – concrete experience, reflective observation, abstract conceptualization, and active experimentation. Different people start their learning in different phases, and rely more heavily on certain phases, following individual natural tendencies.

The Kolb inventory scores learning preferences and categorizes learners into four styles – diverging, assimilating, converging, and accommodating. Those with the diverging learning style prefer to reflect on their experience before, or even instead of, taking action. They like brainstorming, and collaboration. Those with the assimilating style prefer to take in information, organize it, and develop a logical theory about it. They like to read, think, and reflect. The converging style people use information to make decisions and solve problems. They want a concrete outcome, and are often technical. People who have an accommodating learning style learn best from doing, like to explore new experiences, and tend to be intuitive, relying more on people than data. Knowing what kind of learner you are can help you find work in which you most easily learn, or help you to understand why certain learning situations are uncomfortable for you and find ways to modify your approach. You can strengthen your ability to learn in ways that are less natural for you.

Give yourself permission to explore with a little trial and error. Go ahead and ask the questions you need to ask without worrying about looking like you don't have all the answers, and remind yourself that you're in a learning process. Focus on the task at hand and not on how you think you may be perceived. When you're experiencing self-doubt, remind yourself of your accomplishments and know that the feeling of insecurity will pass. When you're feeling good about yourself, take a moment to pat yourself on the back and realize why you're proud, because you know that feeling will also pass.

When you feel discouraged, keep in mind that you've strived, survived and occasionally thrived, and always kept going. You've met challenges that frightened you and come out on the other side, you've found the discipline to do things you didn't want to do, and you've done some things you loved and done them very well. Some of your most satisfying accomplishments are invisible to others, but have great meaning to you. Think about what you've learned, what you've overcome and what you've achieved. Congratulate yourself for being who you are today, and keep living your own unique and meaningful story with pride.

Find a way to hear that other quiet, comforting voice that tells you you're all right and everything will be ok. Create the time and space for this voice to emerge, because it resides most deeply within you, unlike the other voices that live somewhere near the top of your head. Find the time to be alone doing something that allows your spirit to breathe and quiets your mind. Give your wiser self a chance to come out and help you.

Things You Can Do

- If you're in the middle of a challenging situation, think about where you are on the learning curve.

- Make a list of what you need to learn to succeed at this effort.

- Make a list of the things you do best.

- Make a list of areas you would like to strengthen.

- Think about how you learn best, and what kind of work and environment would be most conducive to your learning style.

Self-Recognition

- Make a list of your accomplishments of which you are most proud.

- Then list the personal qualities you have that made these accomplishments possible.

- Note the most difficult situations in which you've found yourself, and the abilities you used to get through them

- Every once in a while show yourself the same kindness you would show someone else and find the patience to give yourself the time to learn what you need to know next.

WORKING WITH FEAR

True fearlessness is not the reduction of fear, but going beyond fear.

Chogyam Trungpa "Shambala, The Sacred Path of the Warrier"

To fear loss is to be human. You may not think of it as fear - you may think that what you want is more money, more things, more "security", or at least certainly not less. At work this fear can get in your way, sometimes even harm you. It's not fun to live with the anxiety that you'll make a wrong move and fail, or that something will happen that's not under your control and render you helpless; that in the end you could lose everything.

But if you've ever watched a newscast of people picking their way through the remains of a disaster – a fire, a flood, a hurricane, an earthquake – you know that everything can disappear in an instant, including people. Some think that humans are the only creatures who can contemplate their own mortality, but if you've ever watched an elephant funeral on National Geographic, this theory becomes suspect. It's the nature of life itself; it's just easier to accept when it's your garden and not your family.

However when you think it through, the chances of you ending up living in a cardboard box on the street are probably pretty slim. Still you can and will lose sometimes, at least if you're trying to make a difference. You'll make mistakes, and then correct course. And it's quite possible in today's environment that something totally out of your control could change your life.

Maybe the fact that all life by definition is cycling through beginnings and endings is why we fear change and fight so hard to hold on to the way things are now. The trick is to accept that loss is part of life, and to remember that you always survive it, at least while you still have breath. Your real security lies in your ability to adapt creatively to whatever life dishes out rather than to try to control it. That doesn't mean you don't need plans and goals; just that you're mentally prepared to shift gears when needed rather than clinging to what's already past.

Every once in a while you need to do something that frightens you. Most of the time you're pretty content plunking along in your comfort zone at work, that is once you've managed to arrive there. It's so nice to feel relaxed, competent, and respected. It seems like you've earned the right to rest in your area of expertise, which after all, you've worked hard to develop. The trouble is there is an innate, relentless drive to evolve that always catches up with you, whether you want it to or not. If you won't choose the unknown yourself, circumstances will eventually provide it for you. You find yourself facing a task that you have no idea how to accomplish, and there are no escape routes. You wonder how you got yourself into this mess, and how you'll get through it.

The most important thing is to remember that you're not alone. Figure out who can provide the support you need, whether it's information, a pep talk, or real assistance from someone who has the knowledge you're lacking. When you stop and think about it, there is always someone you can go to who will help you, and even just talking to someone about what you have to do can be amazingly effective at reducing your anxiety. (Well, depending on who you talk to.) The beautiful thing is that after you've made it through whatever it was – a presentation in front of 500 people, facilitating a meeting of executives, or bungee-jumping from a cliff – you'll feel really good about yourself.

Find ways to develop the flexibility and faith that survivors always seem to have – whatever works for you. This may include spiritual practices, active preparation to be qualified to do more than one kind of work, physical activity that calms your nerves and makes you feel strong, talking to people who seem to have found the key to retaining their equilibrium. It also doesn't hurt to try to live in the present and enjoy as much of your life as you can.

Of course this takes work and focus, and still the

fears will come and go. But as you courageously navigate through more and more storms, you'll come through stronger and wiser each time. You'll come to understand that you're smart enough and tough enough to be ok no matter what. And that calms the mind.

Things You Can Do

- Choose something you've been thinking about doing but putting off because you're not sure you can pull it off.

- Make list of the people you know who can support you in this effort.

- Make a list of people you don't really know who could provide support.

- Choose someone you trust to discuss your ideas and concerns about your potential project.

- Then start talking to the people on your lists and get feedback on your plan and find out what each will contribute.

- Get going and see what happens. Be prepared to change your ideas and your plan.

- Decide what you'll do for stress relief when needed, and mentally commit to really doing it.

WHAT WILL IT TAKE FOR YOU TO FEEL SAFE?

The English word "courage" has the same etymological root as the French coeur, which means "heart." To have courage, just as to have faith, is to be full of heart. With courage we openly acknowledge what we can't control, make wise choices about what we can affect, and move forward into the uncultivated terrain of the next moment.

Sharon Salzberg, "Faith"

What does it take for you to feel safe enough to enjoy your life? How much stuff do you need to own to feel lucky? How do you deal with the fact that everything is temporary? It's hard when you feel like it's all up to you, and that you need to exert as much control as possible over events. It can be reassuring to remember that you're not alone, and there's only so much you can control anyway.

Jim lies in bed in a cold sweat because he owns only one house and has accumulated only a million dollars in his portfolio. He knows people who have much more, and frankly, he thought he'd be in better shape by this time. At least he finally got the VP position, but he knows that VP's can disappear overnight in his company, and that keeps him awake too. Actually, he's not sure he's really qualified. He worries about his family and feels anxious at work.

Janice loves how there is always somehow one more meal that can be constructed from the contents of her kitchen, even if she hasn't been to the grocery store for a while. She feels a little guilty when she thinks of all those on the earth for whom this is not true. As she looks out her sunny apartment window at the perfect fuchsia orchids she is nurturing on the deck she feels fortunate. She's not crazy about her job, and wishes the pay was better, but looks forward to seeing her colleagues. She likes the way they help each other through their work days. She worries about her friend who got laid off last month.

If Jim owned two more houses and had several more millions of dollars he would still probably not feel safe, or take much satisfaction in what he's accomplished. If Janice loses her job today, while it would be a pretty bad experience, she will probably find a way to believe that things will work out. She has a lot of friends, and although they're not what you would call powerful, she knows they will go out of their way to help her get another job.

The difference between Jim and Janice could be explained by history, psychology, or even brain chemistry, but fundamentally it may be a matter of where they put their faith. Jim thinks he can protect himself in a blanket of material security, but knows it could be ripped off at any moment. Janice acknowledges that there are powerful forces at play, and realizes she needs to stay connected and supportive within her network. She knows she is stronger and safer in community than she is by herself.

No matter what your situation is, there's something you can do that's fundamental to creating more possibilities for your future. You can simplify. A lot of the stress caused by economic uncertainty is related to maintaining the lifestyle you believe you need. But how much style does your life really have if all you do is work or worry about work? You have a lot of great stuff you bought in the good old days, maybe a whole house-full, and more stuff you'd like to get. There's always something newer, better, sexier to want. But you have to maintain it all, possibly with diminished or unstable resources. The house, the cars, all the services you depend on so you can work all the time.

Think about what you really need to feel satisfied. Experiment to see how it feels to own less, to want less. Discover what makes you happy, eases your stress. Start with a values check to determine what is important to you at this point in your life, and create your own rules. A garage sale might be fun – some people report feeling like a weight has been lifted from them as they rid themselves of things they never use and don't need. Better yet, give your furniture and all those clothes you haven't touched for a couple of years to a homeless shelter or career closet for low-income people who need to dress for job interviews.

Dine out no more than once a week and go to the farmers' market on the weekend so there's good food in the house; downsize your living quarters for lower mortgage or rent. And – do you really need multiples of things? Computers, televisions, phones, microwaves, furniture, and tchotchkes in every corner? Replace them with experiences, like a cooking class, learning to play chess, gardening.

Track your expenses and figure out your bottom line. When you whack back your obligations, simplify your environment, and choose activities that have meaning for you and bring you joy and peace, a lot of the craving disappears. Once you know what you really need to enjoy your life you have more flexibility regarding work. You're in better shape to sustain a period of unemployment, and you can offer yourself more choices about the kind of work you can do, and how much of your time you want to spend working. You can create more space and bring more daylight into your life.

Maybe you don't need a job at all. The idea of a portfolio career drawing income from multiple sources has become more attractive as jobs have become less plentiful and secure. You have acquired multiple skills in your life and you can get paid for some of them. Make a list of everything you know how to do that you could charge for. Do some research and find out what the demand is for those services, and the pay. Talk to people who are doing it and google around. If you need a certification, find out how to get it. You might choose one boring skill that can bring in consistent income and one or two others that are more entrepreneurial and have potential.

You can find projects on Guru Employer http://www.guru.com or Freelance Work Exchange http://www.freelanceworkexchange.com . If you want to do administrative work from home virtually, there are now many agencies such as Virtual Admin Pro http://www.virtualadminpro.com. You can sell your art or crafts at Etsy http://www.etsy.com or ArtFire http://www.artfire.com . If you like to write, check out http://jobs.problogger.net/ where there are listings for people who want to blog professionally.

Yes, healthcare is still a major issue, since companies are responsible for providing healthcare. However, you can get coverage if you can be insured by your spouse, if you're young and healthy and can purchase reasonably priced health insurance on your own, if you've lost your job and for the time being have Cobra, or if you're eligible for Medicare. Many temporary agencies now provide benefits, and there are some organizations for independent contractors that offer insurance at group rates such as the Freelancers Union http://www.freelancers union.org. If you run a small business you need only one half-time employee to qualify both of you for group insurance rates.

Your real security lies in who you are and what you know how to do – nobody can take that away from you. It takes courage to make this shift in the way you view your life and your work, and yet it can actually make you feel safer knowing no matter what happens you will find a way.

Things You Can Do

- Do some number crunching and figure out your bottom line. What do you really need to be ok?

- Make a list of your skills and talents. Do some research to find out what they're worth.

- Decide if you want more qualifications or experience in any potentially valuable skillset you have, and research ways to improve your expertise and credentials.

- Keep working if you can, and keep developing your Plan B.

HOLD ONTO YOURSELF

Tie a lure onto your line – a belief, and opinion, a provocative question – then chuck it into the stream and see what bites!

Susan Scott "Fierce Conversations"

Do you tell people what you think at work, or do you believe it's best most of the time to remain silent and let the chips fall where they may? It's true that a lot of the issues will eventually resolve themselves one way or the other, and maybe it's safer to just listen and voice no opinion. Your opinion might not be the right one anyway, or maybe you don't even know for sure exactly what your opinion is.

Sometimes you do have a dog in the fight though, and it's harder to keep your mouth shut when the discussion is about something that's important to you and will impact your work. Still, it could be politically unwise to show your hand without knowing who will win the argument. If some of the personalities involved are aggressive, you worry that retribution will descend upon you for taking an opposing position.

Often other voices at the table are louder, more verbose; there's always somebody who has no problem dominating the discussion whether they're adding value or not. Sometimes you have to interrupt just to get a chance to speak at all. It's easier to look down and appear to be taking notes than to confront the stupid ideas ringing in your ears.

Sometimes it's hard to know what to do. A big project is headed off the rails, but only the people doing the work know this, and the project manager is still smiling and presenting colored success charts to upper management. A co-worker is clearly in over his head but unwilling to admit it, and this is impacting others. You have committed a serious error, and fear the consequences of disclosing it. You need your job; you don't want to rock the boat, but at the same time you have to be able to live with yourself. Can you sacrifice your integrity and self-respect for security? Is your security really at risk or does it just feel like it? Often we exaggerate the potential consequences of an act once we start worrying about it.

You might not be asking as many questions as you'd like to either, because you think you need to look like you know pretty much everything at all times. This is a heavy burden to bear, and can make it hard for you to figure out what's actually going on. This applies not only to projects, plans, and technical information, but perhaps most importantly to what the people around you are really thinking.

You want to look confident, competent, and qualified to do the work you were hired to do. But you're in a changing world with new information coming in every day and shifting goal posts. You need to be quick on your feet, constantly coming up to speed. Asking real questions takes courage, and when done in a sincere effort to better understand what's going on, will usually benefit everyone.

You have a voice, but you may have lost it somewhere along the way. If you've been muffling yourself for a long time, and built up a certain level of frustration, you may be afraid of what will come out of your mouth when you finally do open it. However, if you never get an opportunity to practice, you can't develop skillful means to communicate your ideas. It could be really important one day, and actually, it does matter every day.

You know you have insights that could help – maybe not every moment, but sometimes you can see straight through the barrage of words and agendas to the solution, the right thing to do, the right way to do it. Then when you don't speak, you deprive everyone around you of the benefit of your experience and your expertise.

Both professional and personal maturity rely on you knowing who you are and what you believe in. The clearer you are about your values, the more stable your moral compass. It's through experience that we learn what really matters. If you're not sure of your priorities, it's confusing to sort through your options when faced with a difficult decision. You may think you know yourself, but until you are tested you can't be sure. Each time you act in a way that's true to your principles despite potential risk, you validate your authenticity and manifest the kind of strength that engenders respect.

Give it a shot and start speaking up. Chances are that none of your worst fears will be realized, and you may be surprised to find people approaching you after you have expressed yourself to thank you for having done so. When you speak your truth, you are often speaking the truth for others as well.

Things You Can Do

- The next time you're in a situation where you don't say what you really think, when it's over, take a minute to jot down the things you wish you had said.

- Also note any questions you wish you would have asked.

- In preparation for the next similar situation, note a few things you think are important that will probably come up.

- Promise yourself to voice at least one of these thoughts.

- Then go ahead and do it.

- Afterward think about how it felt and what the reactions were, if any.

If you do this repeatedly, after a while your desire to contribute will overtake your fear of repercussions, and you'll feel freer to speak up when it matters to you.

DIFFICULT CONVERSATIONS

Asking for a raise. Ending a relationship. Giving a critical performance review. Saying no to someone in need. Confronting disrespectful or hurtful behavior. Disagreeing with the majority in a group. Apologizing. At work, at home, and across the backyard fence, difficult conversations are attempted or avoided every day.

Stone, Patton & Heen "Difficult Conversations, How to Discuss What Matters Most"

Sometimes you experience anger at work and wonder what to do with it. In our culture it's usually not ok to express your emotions on the job, but that doesn't stop you from feeling them. Worse, if you stuff your frustration, it can stew in its own juices until it's is way out of proportion. Anger can be a powerful drug that distorts your perception of what's going on.

Ask yourself what's bothering you. Then ask yourself what's *really* bothering you. Sometimes it's difficult to clearly identify the cause while experiencing the effect. You might start out thinking I hate everything about this place and everyone in it, and upon reflection realize that what's at the heart of the matter is that your boss isn't treating you fairly, or a colleague whose work affects yours isn't doing a good job. You might even be angry at yourself for not meeting your own standards.

Identifying the cause is important because once you've done that you can develop a plan to improve the situation. It's infinitely better to deal with it early when your emotions are just beginning to build and you can still think clearly, but even if you've been upset about something for a long time, you can work your way out of it. It's just harder.

You may have been sitting on your frustration for so long that you worry if you speak up you will lose control and do irreparable damage. You have concerns that it will just make things worse, or hurt your image. Maybe you're not sure what stops you, but it just seems easier to avoid the issues, that is, until it no longer does.

You *can* discuss your frustrations with whoever is the source without the world ceasing to spin on its axis. Many people, especially those who have held their feelings very privately and deep, fear the consequences of surfacing the issues that caused them. The repercussions you fear by getting all the cards on the table are probably greatly exaggerated, and possibly dead wrong. In fact, you can benefit both yourself and others by bringing concerns into the open where you can deal with them. Examples of conversations you may be avoiding because you fear the consequences are with:

- a colleague who seems to be throwing obstacles in your way

- someone who isn't delivering what you need to be able to do your work

- a boss who doesn't seem pleased with your performance but doesn't say why

- someone who consistently confronts you in meetings

- someone who seems out to get you

It's especially necessary to confront the issues if you think someone at work is trying to sabotage you. If this person has become a primary focus for you, and you find yourself thinking about this person even when you're not at work, it's probably time to do something about it. If you notice your colleagues' eyes glazing over when you're describing the latest crime your enemy has committed against you, and if your spouse leaves the room to get another glass of wine when you launch into today's tale of woe, you are probably spending too much time and energy on this person.

While you may have built the situation up to be more than it needs to be, it's also possible that your rival really would like to see you fail, or at least not do as well as he does. Competitive environments can create this scenario, as can insecurities. Still, it's smarter to hold your opponent close and get to know him. In The Art of War, Sun Tzu says "....if you know your enemies and know yourself, you will not be imperiled in a hundred battles; if you do not know your enemies but do know yourself, you will win one and lose one; if you do not know your enemies nor yourself, you will be imperiled in every single battle."

Ask yourself if any aspects of the problem are actually professional issues that you might be able to resolve. Surprise your rival; change your approach - open up the lines of communication. Explore her intentions with her, instead of using your negative assumptions to build a case against her. Talking directly about the problem can relieve a lot of tension. One way or the other, chances are you'll need to continue to work with this person.

It's especially difficult to voice the questions you have about other people's reasons and intentions. Questions that rattle around in your head unreleased like "why did you do that?", "what were you thinking?", and "what do you want from me?" When you devise answers to these questions for yourself, with no incoming data, you often veer into negative territory. You *can* ask these questions, if you choose the right circumstances and do it with sincere curiosity. Her response may surprise you. Without exploring the motives and desires of colleagues, we often attribute diabolical intentions where something else entirely is at play. While it does take courage to initiate important conversations, there are skills that can be learned to manage them. An excellent guide is *Difficult Conversations* by Stone, Patton, & Heen of the *Harvard Negotiation Project.*

You can prepare by privately noting the main points you want to make. Often these talks can be introduced with a carefully framed question that points straight at the problem. Once you feel you're ready, you can try to create optimal conditions for the conversation. Don't have these conversations when you're angry - how you say what you say and the energy you contribute to the exchange are at least as important what you say.

Ask for a time to meet – preferably on neutral territory. Approach the conversation with a real desire to understand the other person's perspective, improve the working relationship, and ease the tension. Tell her something about yourself to engender a teaspoonful of trust. See if there's anything you can agree on, any way you can support each other. Let past offenses go. When you take control and try to make things better, they usually do get better.

When you have more information about another person's motives you can look at them through a different lens. When you know more about the reasons for a frustrating situation, you can depersonalize your response and either accept it as it is, or take action to change it. Just seeing each other as human beings battling the same environment and challenges can sometimes be enough. You don't have to love each other; just work together reasonably peacefully. You and she and everyone around you will breathe a big sigh of relief. And you will gain confidence in your ability to create positive change.

Things You Can Do

- Choose someone with whom you have a conflict or with whom you would simply like to have a better working relationship.

- Give careful thought to what you believe you need from that person for things to get better.

- Think about what you can do to improve the situation.

- Contact that person to set up a meeting.

- When you meet, be ready to ask questions and really listen to the answers.

  - Tell the person you want a better working relationship.

  - Find out what s/he believes you need to do to make this happen.

  - Express what you think needs to happen.

- Be prepared to compromise.

- Be prepared to forgive and move on.

HOW TO GET YOUR WAY

All activities should be done with the intentlons of speaking so that another person can hear you, rather than using words that cause the barriers to go up and the ears to close.

Pema Chodron "Start Where You Are"

Do you sometimes feel like no matter what you do you're getting nowhere fast? You may have set certain goals; by the time I'm this age I must have this title, by the time I've reached that age I must have these material goods, this amount of money. A look back on your progress may reveal a winding path whose course often changed through seemingly random events. The vision you once had of a straight and orderly climb to the top (or even to the middle) now seems elusive, possibly lost.

There's a good reason for this, since the entire concept of a career ladder is an illusion. Your life is not limited to a one-dimensional exercise that goes in only two directions – up and down. And an organizational chart is an artificial representation of an organization, usually giving a fairly inaccurate idea of how things actually get done. Kind of like the maps you get in the London Underground that show neat color-coded metro lines, when in fact the whole thing is spaghetti.

Your life is dynamic – a whole evolving experience in which your professional and personal development are inextricably intertwined. And as you may have noticed, everything is not under your control. As hard as you work to create your desired reality, life has a way of making swift and unexpected detours. Your ability to adapt and grow from what life throws in your path is your strongest advantage, allowing you to develop the courage and confidence to face whatever comes next.

Believe it or not, a frustrating job can be the perfect place for you to develop skills that will make you more comfortable and successful right where you are in that imperfect situation, and be highly beneficial to you in the future when you move on. Anything you can learn to do in a really difficult situation to improve things for yourself will stay with you forever and be easier to repeat in a better environment. It takes courage and determination to change things under duress, but doing so can facilitate lasting transformation. The workplace can be a laboratory for you to experiment with new perspectives and different behaviors. You can focus on both short and long-term goals, and use your challenging environment as a playground for your own development. You can figure out what you can get out of it for yourself, and go and get it.

Some of the elements that contribute to your dissatisfaction are no doubt classic and can be found in any job. Other factors causing you stress and draining your energy may be particular to your situation and to your responses to the stressors. Usually there are things you are doing that are making things harder. It's useful to distinguish the problems specific to your situation from those you will find anywhere, but more important to identify what you're doing that's contributing to your unhappiness, since only that is under your control. It's the stuff you will take with you to any job; it tends to follow you around.

It helps to think of an organization as a dynamic, constantly changing network of humans interacting in an attempt to reach some (hopefully) common objectives. It's a living, breathing organism mutating at every opportunity, so it's messy. It's comprised of a random bunch of individuals with different perspectives and ideas about practically everything, and the hierarchy cannot be relied upon for order. It's no wonder it gets frustrating at times.

You can spend a lot of time trying to figure out why some people at work are doing some of the things they're doing – especially when it directly affects you. It's hard when you know how it should all work and yet you have to continue to function amidst inefficient processes, misguided goals, and incompetent co-workers. It's even more annoying when you can clearly see what others should be doing, but can't get them to do it.

The most mystifying acts are those that are

completely unlike anything you would ever do. The most aggravating ones are those that get in the way of your goals and desires. While it's true that it can help to see things from someone else's perspective, sometimes it seems impossible to figure out *what* they're thinking.

The language and concepts of psychology are so embedded in our society that there is a general tendency to believe that if we can just analyze a person or a situation correctly, we can fix it. However, as anyone who has been through therapy can tell you, analysis is not enough. Someone has to do something differently to change things, and the only way you can change what someone else is doing is usually by changing something you are doing.

Coaches often give self-observation assignments to clients to encourage them to develop more self-awareness. This is because although you wish fervently you could change some of the behavior around you, the only behavior you have any real power over is your own. And to know what to change, you have to be able to see yourself from a slightly different angle. To do this, imagine splitting yourself into both an actor and an observer and begin to pay attention to how you're functioning and communicating, how you're feeling at the time, and the effect your actions have on others.

You'll begin to realize that you feel better and get better results with certain types of actions and communications, and it will become less mysterious as to why you feel thwarted and get poor results with other behaviors. Admittedly this can be a bit disorienting at first, and - warning - once you start, there's no going back. Once you're aware that you need to be aware, there doesn't seem to be a way to simply become unaware again. It's worth it though, because it's a way to get to know yourself better, and to break out of the idea you've formed of who you are, which is by now an old story anyway.

Next time a certain person, let's call her Susan, is making you crazy, instead of focusing on how it makes you feel, try concentrating on looking for those moments when Susan's behavior shifts from negative to positive, or at least to a behavior that you prefer. Pay attention to what statements or actions seem to have precipitated the change, either from you or someone else. You're exploring behaviors to find out what works with Susan, rather than trying to understand what makes her tick.

Next look back on various Susan scenarios, and develop a theory about what causes her to respond positively. It's probably not too hard to remember the times you've become exasperated with her and what you were doing or saying at those times. What can be more challenging, and is much more useful, is to note those times when whatever you did worked, and she responded well. It can also be interesting to notice her interactions with others and see what they're doing that works with her.

Then at the next opportunity try a different approach or response to Susan based on what you have come to believe puts her into a positive space. Try more than one thing if necessary, and pay attention to which methods work best with her and are most acceptable to you. You want to preserve your integrity; it's not a matter of manipulation, but rather a more disciplined and intelligent way of managing Susan so the work gets done and both of you are more at ease.

You need to be on your toes to respond to the inherent movement within your organization, and creative to maneuver through it as it evolves. You need to influence others to get what you want, and to do this you have to accept some of their ideas, and let go of some of your own. Set goals for yourself that you can realize, and keep an open mind about how to reach them. Entertain ideas from those around you – brainstorming energizes, and can sometimes produce surprising solutions. Things won't turn out exactly the way you pictured it; events will intervene, compromises will be made. Still, by actively managing skillfully through influence, you'll get your way more often.

Once you begin to smooth your own way with improved communication and influence skills, you may find you enjoy your job more, and you may also find greater success right where you are. But if you feel you've gained an improved mastery over your present situation and still want to move on, you can take your more skillful and successful self somewhere else. It'll work there too.

Things You Can Do

Pick someone with whom you have difficulty working, but is someone whose cooperation you need.

- Notice the times when you and he disagree or can't synchronize your efforts.

- Review your communications with this person, read some old emails and meeting notes, remember conversations.

- Decide what you're going to do differently, in both communications and actions, to discover what works to get this person on your side.

- Commit yourself to trying a different approach.

- Watch yourself when you are interacting and communicating with this person. Try to stick to your commitment.

- If you have a colleague whom you can trust to tell you the truth, as him what he sees when he observes you interacting with your problem person.

- If your first attempt doesn't work, modify it and try again.

- Take note when things begin to improve – remember what you did that worked.

Learning to do this is like gradually strengthening your muscles when you work out – it becomes easier the more you do it. Eventually it becomes almost automatic.

CREATE YOUR OWN REALITY

*In today's more open and empowered organizations
and societies, opportunities for exerting influence and
power abound for those who are willing to accept the
attendant responsibilities and accountabilities.*

B. Kim Barnes "Exercising Influence"

You may feel like you're not sure what your job is
actually supposed to be. You thought you had a good
idea in the beginning, but then it became apparent
that the waters are murkier than you thought.
You've noticed that many roles and responsibilities
all around you are kind of vague, and you don't want
to step on anyone's toes. Mostly you'd like to be sure
that your job is a job that they can't do without, so
for starters it would be good to know what it is
exactly.

The fact is, though, you work in a living, breathing
(hopefully) organism that's continuously changing in
the way that organisms must to survive. As in all of
life, nothing stays the same, so any attempt to nail

down your job, assure that it's safe, and keep it that way is doomed anyway. Instead of being annoyed at the lack of clarity in your environment, you can take advantage of it. Where no one is completely sure who's doing what, there is opportunity.

Once you rid yourself of the idea of having a precisely defined and absolutely necessary function, you can get creative. You can devise a better job for yourself, and what's more, once you know how to do this, you can keep doing it for the rest of your working life. Expand your viewpoint - think about the purpose of your organization, and what it needs to accomplish to succeed. Talk to lots of people with different perspectives about what's missing, or blocking something from happening the way it could.

Then assess your strengths, and most importantly, your interests. What percentage of your work do you like? Which parts of it are actually fun for you – when you're completely absorbed and you look up at the clock and can't believe three hours have gone by because you would have guessed it had been thirty minutes? How can you get more of that? We all have to do things we're not crazy about in our jobs, but a general rule of thumb is that the unappealing stuff shouldn't comprise more than fifty percent of your work, and hopefully less. While it's valuable to develop the discipline to become skilled at tasks that don't play to your strengths, it's joyful when you are completely concentrated doing something you are really good at and love to do. Great athletes and performers experience this – it's called flow.

Mihaly Csikszentmihalyi describes this state

beautifully in his classic *Flow*, The Psychology of Optimal Experience" as "the state in which people are so involved in an activity that nothing else seems to matter." He believes that optimal experiences emerge from a sense of mastery, "a sense of participation in determining the content of life." You stop worrying about what other people think of you and focus on the activity, working toward the goal you want to achieve. And this makes you happy.

You may think that what you get to do at work is totally outside of your control, but unless you're on the assembly line at a chicken plucking factory, this is probably not the case. (And even then, who knows?) First you need to identify those times when you are completely absorbed in your work, oblivious to all the things that normally worry you. This requires self-observation, and mental noting of exactly what you are doing at such times. Once you have pulled this information into consciousness, you can create a plan to bring more of the work you enjoy into your job.

Which potential projects can you identify that energize you when you think about them and inspire you to do some serious thinking about how you would solve the problem? What can you see that needs to be done that isn't being done very well, or isn't being done at all? Who do you know who would want to work on this with you, who has knowledge and insight into the situation?

Start a grass-roots movement and work the crowd - get everyone talking about it. If you are really successful, eventually they won't even remember where it started – it will just seem inevitable. Even if you don't get everything you want, you'll win respect as an influential professional who cares about the organization. You'll have a valuable skill you can use again – maybe somewhere else. Most importantly, you'll have done everything you can to make things better.

Yes, if you get what you want it will mean extra work for a while, because you'll also have to keep doing the job you have (whatever that really is), but if you identify the right problem and can sell your ideas about the need to solve it and your approach, you will probably eventually find yourself in a different and more stimulating job. Often you have a greater ability than you imagine to change your role, or move into a different position in your organization, Once you are clear about how you want to spend your time, you can devise ways to make this possible and at the same time benefit the business. Sometimes you can actually create a job that has never existed before, and once you are in it they can't figure out how they ever did without it before.

Not only that, but you'll be identified as someone who understands the business, who takes initiative, and who can evolve with the organization. *You* become the valuable commodity, rather than your function. In this rapidly changing environment your success and security lie in your ability to assess and adapt to current needs. Not to mention you'll get to work on something you actually like.

Things You Can Do

- Choose something you'd like to change or initiate that would add value. If you have an idea of the kind of work you want to do next, make sure it is related to that and can give you some new knowledge and skills.

- Talk about your idea with a few trusted colleagues and friends to get their opinion and ideas about your potential project.

- Once your idea is more fully formed, share it with a few people whose cooperation you need to realize your goals and get their feedback.

- Put together a description of what you want to accomplish. Use whatever format works best in your environment – email, word doc, power point. Be clear and succinct – use as few words as possible and throw in a few numbers if you can.

  o Articulate the benefits, both hard and soft.

- Find the right place and time to present it and bring some of your fellow conspirators with you if you can. By now they are your supporters.

- Then let people know what you're doing and get started.

THE WEB YOU WEAVE

Enlightenment for a wave in the ocean is the moment it realizes it is water.

Thich Nhat Hanh

Sometimes when you've had a major success at work, you're pretty sure the whole place would collapse without you. Other times, under pressure, you feel like it's all up to you and you're not sure you can pull it off. These are both times when it can be useful to remember that you're not alone.

That may or may not be comforting at first glance, depending on the nature of your organization and its members. Certainly there could be no more random assemblage of humans than those chosen simply for their skills and thrown into the same boat with instructions to row in the same direction. But in fact you are inextricably part of a network through which information and influence flow, with the potential to support your efforts.

Maybe the most important question you can ask yourself when embarking on a challenging new project or encountering difficulties in your work is "who can help me with this?" There isn't much you can actually accomplish alone. Usually you have more potential support than you think you do, both for your goals and for yourself, and it often goes untapped.

We have some idea in this culture that we are supposed to be self-sufficient, independent, and never need anyone's assistance, but that's not how anything actually works. Even the Lone Ranger had Tonto (and Silver). It's easier to offer support and advice than to ask for it, mostly because being the advisor feels like the stronger position. In our society a request for help is often veiled in shame, whereas in many other cultures it is considered the normal course of events, and support networks are carefully managed and highly valued.

It's when you believe that you alone are responsible for your success or failure that you are most vulnerable, whether you're winning or losing. For starters, you aren't alone, even if you wish you were. In spite of the American love for heroes, the idea that you can do it by yourself is a myth and a delusion. Most of us are dependent on others to accomplish our work, and need to understand that part of the job is to learn to identify and leverage those who are valuable resources, and manage those who are not.

The more sophisticated professionals in your environment know this; the most successful have mastered it. They are way past worrying about being perceived as weak, and deliberately identify all the resources available to them, including human ones, and engage them to push their agenda forward. Before you sneer at these "politicians", remember that you also have an agenda, and the more energy and talent you can enlist behind what you are trying to create, change, or improve, the better your chances of pulling it off.

We are all connected, like it or not, and every member of a team or organization affects both the other members and the ultimate outcomes. Just as you need support, you provide support for many others. When everything is going well, look around and notice who is contributing to that success. The more conscious you become of who you want in your network, the better you can cultivate and nurture it. This is equally true in your personal life.

Identify those you already know you can count on and like working with, and remember to show your appreciation. Then think about where you're weak or lack information and make a list of colleagues who are strong in those areas. Work on developing positive working relationships with them. Most people actually like being asked for advice, opinions, information.

Most importantly, everyone needs a small (very small) circle of friends to whom you can express your doubts and fears, and who will respect your need for confidentiality. We all have bad days, and this inner circle is critical. If possible, it's nice when there are one or two people you can confide in at work, because they are in that world with you. But if not, you'll need to find it on the outside.

Once you develop an awareness that you are part of an interdependent network, you can develop skills to maneuver inside it and improve your position within it. You will increase your knowledge of how to make things happen and have a more accurate picture of the way things really work in your organization. You can share both your hits and your misses with your colleagues and spend less time feeling alone. It's hard to find community in our society any more, and work may be the closest you can get to it. It's worth paying attention to, because once you get past the model of the solitary dragon slayer and become skillful at organizational interaction, you can accomplish more. Real leaders are good at this.

Things You Can Do

- Forget the image of networking as standing around awkwardly somewhere you don't want to be with people you don't know and a glass of bad, warm wine in a plastic glass.

- Make a list of people in your organization you would like in your network.

    o Start connecting with them – the best way is to have something to offer, like information or assistance. Invite them to coffee or lunch if it feels ok.

- Make a list of people in your profession outside of your organization you would like in your network.

    o This will probably involve making another list of professional organizations you may want to join and professional events you can attend.

    o Connecting with people you used to work with at other companies is a great place to start. Get together or have a phone chat to catch up and reconnect.

DO YOU THINK YOU'RE A LEADER?

Everyday leaders lead not as white knights out in front of bloody battles, but as normal men and women who speak their truth and seize opportunities to create learning and make a difference where they can.

Debra Meyerson "Tempered Radicals"

You don't need to be the ruler of a country or a CEO to be a leader. There are times when you can lead from wherever you are, whether you're sitting at the top or the bottom of the organization chart. Some people demonstrate natural leadership every day, taking responsibility, encouraging others, and taking the initiative to improve things even when there's an element of risk in doing so.

We tend to think of leaders as those in powerful positions, in a class of their own, but regardless of your position you can make a conscious decision to develop your leadership skills. Leading is an action, not a role; it's not a specific set of behaviors, and

71

doesn't belong to a certain job or personality type.

Leadership requires considering the good of the whole, and not just your own survival. It means widening your lens to see a bigger picture, and doing what you can to make things better – for customers, colleagues, even your boss. That usually involves trying to change things, which is where the risk comes in. But to thrive, organizations need people who stimulate positive changes at all levels.

Most importantly, to lead you need to get to know yourself, and what really matters to you. A strong set of values can eliminate a lot of confusion about when and how to act. In his book *Leadership from the Inside Out* Kevin Cashman advises those who want to develop their leadership skills to focus on gaining self-knowledge. He describes seven categories of self-mastery:

Personal: Explore deeply your personal belief system

Purpose: Ask why and explore how

Change: Learn to trust yourself and focus through change

Interpersonal: Understand the importance of relationships

Being: Learn to access the true self

Balance: Maintain work-life balance

Action: Develop authenticity, true self-expression, and create value

Margaret Wheatley has been writing for years about organizations as self-organizing entities, in which change is generated from within through the exchange of energy between all parts of the organization, and not handed down from the top. In her book *Leadership and the New Science* she says that we create our environment through our intentions, and that all actions affect the entire organization because they are all part of the whole. This is the old story about the flutter of a butterfly's wings reverberating around the world, since everything is connected.

You can decide what matters to you and how you will go about trying to make it happen. Because everything you do has impact, you can do high-quality work, even if the task is not your favorite, you can be someone others rely on, you can share your ideas about how to make things better, and you can show appreciation to those around you for their contributions. You can lead.

Things You Can Do

- Notice who in your organization has leadership qualities you admire. Pay attention to their interactions with others and their actions. If there's no one like this where you are, consider other places you've been and reflect on natural leaders you've known. (And if there really is no one, maybe you need to think about changing jobs.)

- Think about the leadership qualities you'd like to develop in yourself – when and how do you want to lead? Remember you don't need to be in front on a white horse swinging a sabor to lead.

- Choose some areas of your work where you could show more leadership, and make a commitment to do that. And when you do it, notice how it feels, and how others react to your leadership.

MANAGING OTHERS

Leadership is relationship and the relationship is one of service to purpose and service to people.

Kouzes & Posner, "The Leadership Challenge"

Most people who manage others don't much like it and aren't very good at it. You can probably count the truly good managers you've had in your career on one or two fingers. If you're a manager yourself, you might be one of those rare individuals who enjoys leading a group and knows how to do it. Or you might just think you're good at it without knowing how you're perceived by those around you. Sometimes it's hard to know what people really think of you once you have power over their lives.

No doubt the reason there are so many bad managers in the world is because usually at some point the only way to get a promotion and the raise that goes with it is to become a manager. So in most cases it's not exactly a calling, and on top of that there's a lot of inadequate management training out there. Almost anyone can learn to be a better manager, even a good manager, but not by learning a few superficial rules. Some serious self-exploration is required, as well as a sincere desire to develop the careers of others along with your own. Yes, they are your resources, and they're also your responsibility. More than that, once you are a manager, the only way you can succeed is through others.

If you catch yourself saying "my people" you might want to pause for a moment and reflect on what that means. They don't actually belong to you, and if you've been managing for any length of time at all, you probably know that they're not always going to do what you ask them to do simply because of your "authority." So what is your real relationship to them and how can you motivate them to consistently do their best? What can you do to create an environment that encourages collaboration, cooperation and high performance?

Beyond routine obligations, articulate a mission for your group that improves something, or creates something, and requires focus and some creative thinking. Naturally it needs to map to your organization's goals, but it should be specific to your group's function and really worth doing. Give direction about what is valuable to the rest of the organization and let them determine exactly what they're aiming for and how they'll achieve it. Brainstorm together to determine the desired outcomes and strategy.

Give clear, honest one-on-one feedback frequently to

each person about what he needs to do to improve his work so there are no surprises at the annual reviews. If someone on your team is failing, confront that fact with him as early as possible and make sure there's no doubt about what he needs to do to get back in sync. See what you can do to help him – often when people are thrashing it's because they're unclear about their responsibilities or simply in the wrong position.

Meet individually with each member of your staff as often as is reasonable and learn what they want for themselves and how you can help them progress. Help each one define a path to progress within the organization and identify next steps. Everyone needs something to shoot for. Let the people who work for you know that you appreciate their efforts, and recognize excellence publicly when it occurs. Above all, model the values and work ethic you want to see from the group.

Managing down is probably the easiest form of management, and is usually the first thing a potentially good manager masters. Once comfortable in that role, many managers believe they know what they're doing - a classic error. Yes, the people who report to you want you to guide and support them, but just as importantly they see you as their connection to the larger organization, and their representative in that world. Many companies have become somewhat more loosely organized in recent years rendering the influence you have with your peers extremely important. Often you need to negotiate with them for shared resources, not to mention they may be consulted for feedback on your performance.

Almost nothing creates more negative energy for your group than when you enter into a conflict with another manager that is not quickly resolved. Don't kid yourself – everyone who reports to you and everyone who reports to the other manager can see what's going on; they're all talking about it, and fear it will impede their work. Not to mention you begin to look like a liability to them rather than an asset. And if it goes on long enough one of them will go behind your back to talk to your boss about the situation, not wanting to confront you directly but believing it must be done for the good of the whole.

You need to work reasonably smoothly with your peers, even those with difficult personalities and unsavory agendas – especially those. There are skills you can develop to achieve this, and acquiring them will require some work on yourself. You can pretend to be neutral, patient, and cooperative but that won't last long under stress. It's more effective to develop a perspective as well as some skillful tactics that allow you to remain relatively calm, think clearly, and find the patience to work through disagreements and obstacles. It's important to communicate frequently and well with your peers even if their work is not directly involved with yours because you need to build the trust and lasting relationships that will help you succeed.

Entertain for a moment the possibility of detached engagement. The fundamental idea of detached engagement is that it's possible to care deeply and still retain a certain detachment, placing the focus on what you want to achieve rather than on yourself. You want a good outcome, but realize that your plans will probably need to change. You know you'll have to work with people who for different reasons aren't coming through the way you need them to, so rather than wasting time in anger, figure out how to compensate. Stop worrying about your image and find creative solutions to keep your project moving forward.

And then there's "managing up." Some people are very good at this right from the get-go, but for others this is the most difficult of all. Needless to say, when you don't have a good relationship with your boss, you and everyone associated with you feels in jeopardy. Since usually you have no choice about who you report to, you need to seriously apply all your brainpower to assure that you can work well with your manager, regardless of who it is. Whether your manager is a bully or a wimp, sharp as a tack or mentally challenged, wise and compassionate or completely oblivious to the needs of others, you need to figure out how to get this person to do what you want her to do.

This is not to be confused with sucking up, which as you may have noticed some of your colleagues have chosen as their path to success. If you think it's disgusting to watch, imagine what it's like to be on the receiving end of it – at least if the person receiving the sucking up has the tiniest amount of self-awareness. At any rate, just smiling, agreeing, and pandering amount to a temporary solution at best.

Forget the ideas you have about who someone needs to be to have the right to manage you, and how they need to act, and study your boss closely to see what you need to do to work with her. Of course there are situations where you might actually decide you need to just get a different job; sadly that is the number one reason people do change jobs – to get away from a bad manager. But usually you can find a way to get along with her, and sometimes you can develop a stimulating and satisfying partnership.

Find out what your manager needs so she can trust you, rely on you, and believe she needs you. This can be a challenge, since there are as many kinds of bosses as there are people, and sometimes even she doesn't know what she wants. The micromanager feeds off detail, while the hands-off manager wants you to take the ball and run with it and just give her the information she needs when she needs it. You need to find the right balance.

Don't try to do this analysis alone – ask others who have worked with her for a long time. Ask *her* what she needs from you, and ask enough questions so she's forced to be clear and precise. Don't be afraid to document these understandings in follow-up emails and brief status updates. The other part of this equation is that you also need to let your manager know what she needs to do for you. Let her know what information and support you need from her to be able to do a good job and make her look good in the process.

You won't regret the time and energy you put into understanding your boss and consciously developing a strategy for supporting her in a way that's comfortable for her and works for you too. You can avoid a lot of misunderstanding by making mutual expectations explicit. It's professional, respectful, and can get you where you want to go.

When you put yourself in a leadership position, you need to lead to the best of your ability. The more awareness you have about what motivates those around you and the more clarity you have about yourself and the areas in which you need to grow, the better leader you will be. Learn all you can about influencing others and effective communication. Find out what you need to do for yourself to be able to maintain your energy and equilibrium, especially under stress, and make time to give yourself what you need. Your focused intelligence and skillful interactions will help you both professionally and personally, and be of great benefit to your organization.

Things You Can Do

- Set aside some time and plan a process for working with your team to develop an overarching mission for the group.

  o Meet regularly to identify specific outcomes and develop strategy.

  o Continue meeting to assess progress and make necessary modifications.

- In your one-on-one meetings with direct reports include discussion about their futures and provide some direction as a mentor.

- Choose a peer with whom you would like to have a better working relationship and find ways to spend some time with that person and get to know him and what he values. This can comfortably be related to mutual professional efforts and interests.

- Meet with your boss and ask what she would like to see more of from you, and what she would like to see less of. Tell her how she can help you be more effective – be specific about what you need from her.

- Find out where you need to improve to be a better manager – a 360 review that gives you feedback from those above, under, and around you can be very useful in determining this. Then find support to learn the new skills you need. A good coach can be invaluable in this process, but if that's not possible, find some good classes and read some books on the subject, and talk to people who seem to have mastered the skills you want to acquire.

YOUR MISSION

To have a firm persuasion, to set out boldly in our work, is to make a pilgrimage of our labors, to understand that the consummation of work lies not only in what we have done, but who we have become while accomplishing the task.

David Whyte "Crossing the Unknown Sea: Work as a Pilgrimage of Identity"

Does your work have meaning? Of course it's meaningful to keep a roof over your head and take care of your family, but is there more to your work than that? This question may be easier to answer if you work in an organization whose primary focus is social benefit, but even there over time you can become less certain that your work is having the impact you thought it would. And if you are in a large corporation whose primary goal is to churn out widgets and maximum profits, you have mornings when you get up and wonder, what's the point?

Your ambition can keep you going to some extent –

In the beginning it looks like it's all in front of you. If you work smart and compete to win, there's no reason you can't make it happen for yourself. You're willing to take on hard stuff, including things you don't really like to do, because it's all part of your plan. It's moving you toward your goal to gain status, recognition, and, of course, lots of money. As long as you're grabbing for the next brass ring you're too busy to bother with an existential dilemma.

But once you've achieved what you set out to do, or have run into your own brick wall or glass ceiling, ambition is no longer the fuel that powers you. Some people never ask themselves what meaning their work has until they find their kids have grown and they have everything they really need. So - now what? Granted, for some people making money really is their mission, and they love every aspect of the game of business, especially keeping score. But although they pretty much rule our culture, they are a small minority.

Ambition is a powerful fuel, and can enable you to do things you would never naturally do. But what about when the game doesn't stimulate you much anymore? You feel deflated, a little lost, and start asking yourself tough questions about what you really want to do. Along the way you've learned more about what you like to do, and you're beginning to realize that you don't have enough of it in your work.

You're experiencing a classic phase of your own evolution when this happens. You can choose to ignore it, because it's frightening to think of what will happen if you pursue this line of thought. And you might have compelling reasons to block this new understanding out of your mind, like the mortgage, college tuition, and all those toys you want to keep buying. But if you let yourself think about how you want to spend what's left of your life and who you want to hang out with, you could end up needing to make some changes.

Regardless of your skills and experience, and the logical pro and con lists you make before you make a career move, there's more to you than your cerebral cortex. The "more" part of yourself often gets ignored, or goes unseen for many years. If it doesn't get fed, it gets hungrier and hungrier and begins to gnaw away at any sense of accomplishment you have. Something is missing. Ambition can transform itself from a desire to succeed to a desire to serve, to bring value to others. Or a desire to create, for the joy of bringing something into existence that wouldn't be there otherwise. It could be as simple as finding a way to be productive that feels more right, more like you, that doesn't feel like work.

It can take time to discover what's important to you. Some people seem to be born knowing what they need to do, but for most of us the haze only begins to clear after much experimentation and downright thrashing around. If it makes you nervous to even think about having a mission, it's because once you know what it is, you'll have to do something about it.

It's not just a matter of choosing between corporate and non-profit work, but of deliberately seeking to find a way to work that fits with what you value. This may mean finding an organization whose work you find important and meaningful, or it could be as basic as the decisions you make about how you communicate and support those around you wherever you work. Your mission can be to feed hungry people or simply to model a competent and compassionate work ethic while refinancing mortgages. If you contribute positive energy to your exchanges with colleagues, customers, and clients, and strive to improve things, then your work has meaning whether you are the CEO of a multinational corporation or are serving burgers at McDonalds.

Take some time to think about what your mission would be if you dared to have one. Warning – this knowledge does tend to haunt you once you have it. It begins to guide your steps and influence your decisions, both the big ones and all the little ones you make all day long. Still, the stronger you hold it in mind, the more whole you feel – like something that was missing has been found, and fallen into place. Maybe if you look for it, you'll find a path that feels strangely familiar, as if you had passed it by before, and it has been waiting all this time for you to step onto it

Things You Can Do

- Spend time reflecting on what your mission truly is.

- Write it down. Keep working on this till it feels right. This is harder than it sounds, and can take a while.

- Think about the work environments that would support your personal mission.

- If you know anyone with a similar mission, talk to them about yours.

- Decide what needs to change in your life for you to realize your mission.

WHAT'S YOUR DREAM NOW?

I have heard it all my life
A voice calling a name I recognized as my own.

Oriah Mountain Dreamer "The Call"

What did you want to be when you were little – a pro ball player, a great American novelist, a movie star? Did you picture yourself as one of those important people holding the world in the palms of their hands and always in the news? Or maybe you were content to imagine yourself as a wealthy business owner flying everywhere in your private jet. Quite possibly you're doing something a little different from what you imagined back then.

Some days when you have your grownup hat on it feels just fine. But there are quiet moments when skies are gray and you wonder if you blew it. You have a select number of memories about decisions you made, paths you didn't take, opportunities you didn't recognize at the time. If only you could have seen clearly and had the discipline to create a plan that would take you to your chosen destination.

But life intervened in its usual messy, organic way and a series of seemingly random events brought you to this place and time. In the process you've become someone different from the self who dreamed those past dreams. Everything you've done has taught you and formed you and changed you. Still, there is something powerfully haunting and nostalgic about that young voice that sometimes still whispers "It was supposed to be different."

If you woke up tomorrow morning and found yourself living one of those early dreams, you might be surprised to discover that it's no longer what you want. A different you wanted that. So the question is - what's your dream now? First you have to stop beating yourself up for not achieving what you can actually only imagine would have been just perfect for you. Then you should congratulate yourself on what you have managed to do – survive and even thrive through life's changing currents, learning, adapting, and renewing your faith that whatever happens, you can deal with it. Remind yourself of the value of so much of what you have done with your life. Even if your dressing room doesn't have a star on it, you still have the leading role in your life.

Reflect on what dream you might want to entertain now and think about what you would need to do to make it actually happen. No matter where we are in our lives, we need something in front of us. Old unrealized dreams are freighted with regret and belong to a self that no longer exists. New unrealized dreams belong to you now and are filled with hope.

Some dreams are meant to stay dreams, and serve mostly to lull you to sleep at night, while others are pleading with you to enter your real life. It can be hard to distinguish between your fantasies and those hopes and desires you can actively pursue. Thinking about living on a boat and sailing around the world is a great escape, especially if you've never been on a boat and have no idea what it would really be like. Imagining yourself running your own small business involving an interest you've had for a long time would probably be more stimulating and actually keep you awake. That's your first clue.

We're often dissatisfied with the status quo and at the same time fear the unknown, so hesitate to go after something that will change our lives. What if you fail? What if you succeed and find it to be less satisfying than you thought it would be? But your world is changing all around you every moment regardless of what you do, so any attempt to hold onto the safety of what you know is futile.

You can get stuck in spite of your desire for change, mulling ideas ranging from having your own bakery to running a hedge fund. You need to go through a process of sorting through your skills, experiences, and values to make a choice. Begin by looking at everything you've ever done – not just your work experience, but other experiences you've had that were important to you. If nothing else, this will make you feel pretty good about all you've done and learned so far.

Think back and recapture the different dreams you had about what you would do when you "grew up" and notice when experiences you sought were related to these earlier passions. Sometimes it can be hard to remember what mattered so much earlier on because you've stuffed it so far down to focus on simply making a living. It's good to bring it back because it's part of who you are. Examine your current values; they can change over time. Identify everything you most want in your life and your work, and compare that to what you have now.

Think big, run through all your fantasies, and then start whittling away the pipe dreams to see what path you'd like to take to get work that would be more satisfying, more connected to your natural talents and desires. You don't need to identify a specific job at this point; a general direction can get you started. Looking for the perfect work is kind of like looking for the perfect mate; you could wait a long, long time. It's easier to think of it as the thing you want to do next. If you suffer from the delusion that everyone but you has a master plan and knows exactly where they are headed, you are tormenting yourself unnecessarily.

First get some real data to inform your decision. Identify people who are doing the work you want to do, and ask them to meet with you. Usually people are flattered by your interest and are happy to do this. Ask good questions – find out what they like and don't like about their work. Ask them to describe a typical day. Ask what their job means to them. (While you are doing this, you are also quite naturally networking, of course.)

Go online and see what's available in this line of work; search creatively with different combinations of search words. Notice the organizations posting the jobs that interest you and keep the better job descriptions for further study and use in redesigning your resume when you're ready. Indeed.com pulls in jobs from almost all job search engines, so it's convenient one-stop shopping. For non-profit work opportunityknocks.com is better.

Experience at least some aspects of your dream to see what it feels like when you bring it into the real world. If you think you want to run a restaurant, work in one on weekends for a while. If you're thinking about going back to school for a specific degree, take one class in that subject. Trying things on for size makes them real, and gives you the information you need to choose an exciting new goal.

From this research, decide what you need to do to qualify for your new work. What courses do you need to take, and where can you get them either online or in the evening? Books you can read? Is there some volunteer work you could do that could give you some appropriate experience? Idealist.org lists many interesting volunteer opportunities. If you need a certification or even a degree, find out where you can get that, how long it will take, what it will cost, what financial aid is available to you. If you're really determined, you can do it.

Once you've engaged and there is real action in your plan, you'll feel renewed hope for your future, and a surprising amount of energy to do all you need to do to get there. Oddly enough, when you start taking even small steps on a new path, the old job doesn't seem so bad anymore, because you no longer feel like you're stuck there. You know you can go and get something better if you really want to.

Things You Can Do

- Use your journal to track your thoughts, research and plans.

- Log what you like and don't like about your current job.

- List the skills you have developed from your experiences, including those that seem minor, or not work-related.

- Review your education, including the times when you got off the track.

  ○ What did you study that was truly compelling? Is it anywhere in your life now?

  ○ What about any courses you took as an adult just because you wanted to know more about something?

- List the elements and qualities you want in your life and your work, and prioritize them – putting them in order is a very interesting and challenging exercise.

  ○ What's working for you now, and what's missing?

- When you have some ideas about the direction you'd like to go in, start your research.

  ○ You can stay open to several different options while doing this.

- Once you've narrowed your path, document a

plan for getting there.

o Remain alert and flexible enough to continue to consider new information and modify your plan as you pursue it.

ABOUT THE AUTHOR

Kathleen Marvin is an experienced and insightful career development coach for people who want to improve their communication, influence, and leadership skills, make a career change, or simply find more balance in their lives.

She has coached professionals from numerous technology companies including Adobe, Cisco, Sun Microsystems, Autodesk, NetApp, and IBM as well as non-profit executives, small business owners, and entry-level employees. Kathleen was an executive at Adobe, Apple (Claris), Autodesk, and Sun Microsystems, and has an international business background. She has lived and worked in Europe and Latin America, worked with Asia, and is conversational in French, Portuguese and Spanish.

Kathleen has a B.A. in Psychology from Antioch University and an M.A. in Organizational Psychology from John F. Kennedy University. She is a Professional Certified Coach trained at New Ventures West, which is accredited by the International Coaching Federation.

www.working-life.biz

May you be filled with loving kindness

May you be well

May you be peaceful and at ease

May you be happy

Made in the USA
Charleston, SC
03 November 2011